The Teachings in Pablo Marçal

"A JOURNEY TOWARDS PROSPERITY AND SUCCESS"

Elean Bolandine

Campinas, São Paulo, Brasil

Copyright © **2024**
2ª edição (English version)

All rights to the work
The Teachings in Pablo Marçal
"A Journey Towards Prosperity and Success"

Reserved to the author
Elean Bolandine (1977)

Cover art – *Elean Bolandine*

All rights reserved. This book/ebook or any part thereof may not be reproduced or used in any way without express written permission from the author or publisher, except for the use of brief quotations in a review of the book/ebook.

The Teachings in Pablo Marçal

"A Journey Towards Prosperity and Success"

Elean Bolandine

summary

Introduction:

Chapter 1: The Journey of Pablo Marçal

- Introduction to the life and career of Pablo Marçal as a leader in branding.
- The fundamental principles that guided him to success in business.

Chapter 2: The Power of Self-Knowledge

- Exploration of Pablo Marçal's belief in self-knowledge as a basis for personal and professional growth.
- Practical exercises for readers to start discovering more about themselves.

Chapter 3: Building Your Personal Brand

- The secrets behind building a strong personal brand, as taught by Pablo Marçal.
- Practical tips for identifying and communicating your authenticity.

Chapter 4: Digital Strategies for Success

- A dive into the digital methods recommended by Pablo Marçal to achieve success in business.
- Examples of effective digital marketing strategies.

Chapter 5: Future Vision and Innovation

- How Pablo Marçal sees the future of business and the importance of innovation.
- Insights into how to stay relevant in a world constantly changing.

Chapter 6: Prosperity Mindset

- The mental attitudes necessary to attract prosperity, as taught by Pablo Marçal.
- Strategies for cultivating an abundance mindset in all areas of life.

Chapter 7: The Importance of Resilience

- Lessons on resilience and overcoming challenges, inspired by the experience of Pablo Marçal.
- Stories of perseverance and how to transform adversity into opportunities.

Chapter 8: Wealth: More Than Money

- Reflections on the true meaning of wealth beyond the financial aspects.
- How to achieve an abundant life in all areas, not just in the material.

Chapter 9: The Role of Education and Lifelong Learning

- The importance of education and personal development on the journey towards success, according to Pablo Marçal.
- Recommendations for books, courses and resources to expand knowledge.

Chapter 10: Leadership and Entrepreneurship

- Insights into effective leadership and successful entrepreneurship based on the experience of Pablo Marçal.
- Leadership principles that can be applied in different contexts.

Chapter 11: Social Impact and Corporate Responsibility

- Pablo Marçal's vision of the role of companies in society and the importance of assuming social responsibilities.
- Examples of corporate initiatives that make a difference in the world.

Chapter 12: Implementing the Teachings of Pablo Marçal

- A practical guide for readers to apply Pablo Marçal's teachings in their own lives and businesses.
- Strategies to transform knowledge into action and achieve tangible results.

Epilogue
- Towards a New Journey

This book offers an immersion in the teachings and philosophies of Pablo Marçal, providing readers with a source of inspiration and guidance to achieve prosperity and success in your own journeys.

Introduction

A Journey Toward Prosperity and Success

Dear reader,

It is with immense gratitude and enthusiasm that I welcome you to this inspiring book, "The Teachings of Pablo Marçal: A Journey Towards Prosperity and Success".

This book is the result of years of reflection, experience, and learning, and it is an honor to share these teachings with you. Throughout my own entrepreneurial and personal development journey, I have found Pablo Marçal to be an inexhaustible source of inspiration and wisdom. His unique approach to branding, leadership and self-awareness transformed not only the way I do business, but also my outlook on life.

In this book, you will find a careful synthesis of Pablo Marçal's teachings, presented in an accessible and practical way.

From the fundamentals of branding to the secrets to prosperity and success, each page is an invitation to a journey of self-discovery and growth.

But this book goes beyond simply imparting knowledge. It is a call to action.

As you absorb the insights and strategies presented here, you will be challenged to apply them to your own life and business. True transformation comes from deliberate, consistent action, and this book is here to guide you along that path.

As you delve into the pages that follow, I invite you to open your mind and heart to new possibilities.

This is the beginning of an extraordinary journey toward realizing your wildest dreams and creating a life of purpose, passion and true impact.

May this book be a beacon of light on your path, illuminating the path to a life of prosperity and success beyond your wildest dreams.

With gratitude and expectation,

Elean Bolandine

Chapter 1:
The Journey of Pablo Marçal

Pablo Marçal is a name that resonates in the contemporary business world as one of the most prominent leaders in the field of branding.

His journey to the top was not only marked by success, but also by a deep understanding of the fundamental principles that govern the business world.

Born in a small country town, Pablo Marçal has always demonstrated a unique vision and incomparable determination from a young age.

His passion for entrepreneurship and creating something meaningful drove him to seek knowledge in areas such as marketing, psychology and technology, preparing him for the challenges that lay ahead.

Throughout his career, Pablo Marçal faced countless obstacles and setbacks, but it was his resilience and his ability to learn from each experience that led him to earn his place as one of the most renowned digital strategists today.

Its core principles are simple but powerful: authenticity, innovation and resilience.

These were the pillars on which he built his business empire, remaining true to himself and the values he considers essential.

In this chapter, we'll explore Pablo Marçal's journey from his humble beginnings to his rise as one of the greatest leaders in branding, while delving into the principles that guided him to business success.

Get ready for an inspiring journey around the world from a visionary entrepreneur who defied the odds and left his indelible mark on the world of business.

With a mind hungry for knowledge and tireless determination, Pablo Marçal began his entrepreneurial journey with few resources other than his own passion and vision.

In the eyes of many, his ambition might have been considered unrealistic, but for Pablo, it was the only viable option.

From an early age, he understood that success would not be achieved with technical skills or theoretical knowledge alone, but rather with a deep understanding of the ever-evolving world of business and human psychology.

He dove headfirst into studies, absorbing everything he could about marketing, branding and digital strategies, always with a keen eye on emerging trends and market needs.

Over the years, Pablo Marçal has built a solid reputation as a visionary strategist,
capaz de antecipar mudanças e adaptar-se rapidamente a novas circunstâncias.

Sua abordagem única para branding, baseada na autenticidade e na conexão emocional, logo chamou the attention of large companies and entrepreneurs looking for guidance.

However, the path to success was not without its challenges.

Pablo faced moments of doubt and uncertainty, moments when it seemed like his ambitions were beyond his reach.

But it was his unwavering resilience and ability to learn from every setback that drove him forward, turning every obstacle into an opportunity for growth and empowerment.

Today, Pablo Marçal is recognized not only as a leader in branding, but also as a mentor and inspiration to thousands of aspiring entrepreneurs around the world.

His journey is a testament to the power of self-knowledge, persistence and an unwavering belief in the human potential to achieve great things.

In the next chapters, we will explore more deeply the principles and teachings that shaped Pablo Marçal's path and discover how we can apply them to our own journeys towards success in business and in life.

,

14

Chapter 2:
The Power of Self-Knowledge

Pablo Marçal has always emphasized the crucial role of self-knowledge in personal and professional development.

For him, the journey to success begins with a deep understanding of who we are, our values, beliefs and motivations.

It is this solid foundation that enables us to make conscious decisions, establish goals aligned with our essence and face challenges with confidence and clarity.

Exploring self-knowledge is not just an intellectual exercise, but an emotional and spiritual journey that leads us to discover our true selves. Pablo Marçal believes that only when we know ourselves completely can we reach our full potential and live a meaningful and fulfilling life.

In this chapter, we will delve into the practices and principles that Pablo Marçal advocates for cultivating self-knowledge:

1. **Daily Reflection:**
Set aside time every day to reflect on your experiences, thoughts and emotions.
Write down your reflections in a journal or notebook to track your progress over time.

2. **Deep Questioning:**
Ask yourself powerful questions like "Who am I?" and "What really matters to me?" Explore your answers with honesty and curiosity.

3. **External Feedback:**
Seek feedback from trusted friends, family and colleagues about your qualities, strengths and areas for improvement.
Be open to constructive criticism and use it as opportunities for growth.

4. **Mindfulness Practices:**
Practice mindfulness techniques, such as meditation and conscious breathing, to cultivate mindfulness and awareness of the present moment.

5. **Constant Self-Assessment:**
Regularly evaluate your progress against your goals and values.
Make adjustments as needed to ensure you are following the path that best resonates with your inner truth.

6. **Pattern Identification:**
Observe the patterns of thought, behavior and emotions that arise in different situations in your life.
Identifying these patterns can reveal valuable insights into your tendencies and preferences.

7. **Exploration of Values:**
Take time to identify and define your personal values.
Ask yourself which principles are most important to you and how these values influence your choices and actions.

8. **Analysis of Past Experiences:**
Reflect on your past experiences, both positive and negative. What did you learn from these experiences? How have they shaped who you are today? Use these reflections to inform your future decisions.

9. **Creative Visualization:**
Practice creative visualization, imagining your ideal self and the life you want to create for yourself.
Use all of your senses to make this visualization as vivid and realistic as possible.

10. **Positive Self-Talk:**
Cultivate positive, compassionate self-talk.

Instead of criticizing or judging yourself, practice self-compassion and encouragement, reminding yourself that you are worthy of love and acceptance, just as you are.

These practical exercises are just the beginning of the journey of self-knowledge.

As you commit to these practices and delve deeper into your own essence, you will discover a wealth of insights and discoveries about yourself.

Pablo Marçal reminds us that self-knowledge is the key to unlocking our unlimited potential and achieving a life of fulfillment and purpose.

In the next chapters, we'll explore how these insights can be applied in the business world and beyond, empowering us to create a truly meaningful and fulfilling life.

Chapter 3:
Building Your Personal Brand

Building a strong personal brand is essential to stand out in an increasingly competitive and connected world.

Pablo Marçal is a master of this art and shares with us the secrets behind building an authentic and impactful personal brand.

1. **Identifying Your Authenticity**

The first step to building a personal brand is knowing yourself.

Pablo Marçal teaches us to delve deep into our essence, identifying our values, passions and strengths.

By understanding what makes us unique, we can build a brand that is true and genuine.

2. **Defining Your Unique Value Proposition**

Each of us has something special to offer the world.

Pablo Marçal encourages us to identify our unique value proposition, what differentiates us from others and makes us unforgettable.

This could be a special skill, a unique perspective, or even our life story.

3. **Creating a Captivating Narrative**

A strong personal brand is built on a captivating narrative.

Pablo Marçal teaches us how to tell our story in an authentic and moving way, highlighting our experiences, achievements and values.

Powerful storytelling helps us connect with others on an emotional level and build lasting relationships.

4. **Communicating Consistency**

Consistency is key to building a strong personal brand.

Pablo Marçal reminds us of the importance of communicating our authenticity coherently in all aspects of our lives - from our in-person interactions to our online presence.

This means maintaining a consistent visual language, a clear message and a confident stance in everything we do.

5. **Building Authentic Relationships**

Ultimately, a strong personal brand is built on authentic relationships.

Pablo Marçal teaches us to cultivate genuine connections with each other by showing genuine interest, listening carefully, and being truly ourselves in every interaction.

6. **Developing an Impactful Online Presence**

In today's digital world, a strong online presence is essential to building an effective personal brand.

Pablo Marçal guides us on how to create social media profiles that convey our authenticity and value proposition in a clear and consistent way.

This includes creating relevant content, engaging with the community, and maintaining a professional and authentic image online.

7. **Investing in Personal Development**

A strong personal brand is not just about how we present ourselves to the outside world, but also about our continued personal growth and development.

Pablo Marçal encourages us to invest in our education and skills, seeking learning and growth opportunities that help us achieve our goals and enhance our personal brand.

8. **Receiving and Incorporating Feedback**

To build an authentic personal brand, it's essential to receive feedback from others and be open to constructive criticism.

Pablo Marçal teaches us to value the opinion of others and to use feedback as an opportunity for learning and continuous improvement.

This helps us refine our personal brand and become even more authentic and impactful.

9. **Being Consistent and Adaptable**

Building a strong personal brand requires consistency while being open to adapting to changes in the environment.

Pablo Marçal shows us how to find the balance between maintaining an authentic identity and being flexible enough to adjust to new circumstances and opportunities that arise in our lives.

10. **Celebrating Authenticity**

Finally, Pablo Marçal reminds us of the importance of celebrating our authenticity and being proud of who we are.

Building a strong personal brand is not just about achieving external success, but also about finding meaning and personal fulfillment in our journey.

By following Pablo Marçal's teachings and implementing these practical tips, we can build a strong and authentic personal brand that helps us achieve our goals and live a truly meaningful and fulfilling life.

In the next chapters, we will explore how to apply these principles in the business world and in the search for professional success.

24

Chapter 4:
Digital Strategies for Success

In today's digital world, business success often depends on the ability to effectively utilize digital strategies.

Pablo Marçal is a visionary in this field and shares with us the strategies he recommends to achieve success in online business.

1. **Building a Consistent Online Presence**

A strong online presence is essential for success in digital business.

Pablo Marçal encourages us to create a professional website and maintain active profiles on social networks relevant to our target audience.

This includes creating quality content and regularly engaging with followers to build a strong online community.

2. **Relevant and Valuable Content Marketing**

Content marketing is one of the most effective strategies for attracting and engaging customers online.

Pablo Marçal teaches us how to create relevant and valuable content that resonates with our target audience, providing useful information, solving problems and inspiring action.

3. **SEO Strategies (Search Engine Optimization)**

To ensure that our content is found online, it is essential to optimize it for search engines.

Pablo Marçal guides us on SEO best practices, including keyword research, optimizing titles and meta descriptions, and creating high-quality, relevant content.

4. **Email Marketing Strategies**

Email marketing continues to be a powerful tool for reaching and nurturing leads.

Pablo Marçal shows us how to create effective email campaigns, segment our contact list based on interests and behaviors, and deliver personalized and relevant content for each stage of the buying cycle.

5. **Social Media Marketing**
Social media is an essential platform for engaging and building customer relationships.

Pablo Marçal teaches us how to create an effective social media strategy by identifying the right platforms for our target audience, creating engaging content, and actively interacting with followers.

6. **Data Analysis and Performance Metrics**

Finally, Pablo Marçal reminds us of the importance of constantly monitoring and analyzing the performance of our digital strategies.

This allows us to identify what is working well and what needs to be adjusted, ensuring that we are always optimizing our actions to obtain the best possible results.

By implementing these digital strategies recommended by Pablo Marçal, we can position our businesses for success online, effectively reaching and engaging our target audience and driving growth and profitability.

7. **Influencer Marketing**
An increasingly popular strategy in the digital world is influencer marketing.

Pablo Marçal shows us how to identify and collaborate with influencers who have relevance and credibility with our target audience.

This could include partnerships for sponsored posts, participation in events, or even joint product development.

8. **Remarketing and Retargeting**
Remarketing and retargeting are powerful techniques for reaching people who have already interacted with our website or online content.

Pablo Marçal guides us on how to set up effective remarketing campaigns, displaying personalized ads to users who have shown interest in our products or services, thus increasing the chances of conversion.

9. **Marketing Automation**
Automating marketing processes can save time and resources while enabling more personalized and relevant communication with customers.

Pablo Marçal introduces us to marketing automation tools, which can be used to segment leads, send automated emails with
base em comportamentos do usuário e nutrir leads ao longo do funil de vendas.

10. **Investment in Online Advertising**

Finally, Pablo Marçal highlights the importance of investing in online advertising to expand reach and increase brand visibility.

This can include ads on social networks like Facebook and Instagram, search ads on Google, video ads on YouTube, and more.

It guides us on how to create effective advertising campaigns by setting clear objectives, segmenting the target audience appropriately, and tracking performance for continuous optimization.

By applying these digital strategies together, we can create a robust and impactful online presence that allows us to effectively reach and engage our target audience, driving growth and success for our business.

In the next chapters, we will explore concrete examples of how companies from different sectors and sizes have used these strategies to achieve impressive results in the digital world.

Chapter 5
Future Vision and Innovation

Pablo Marçal: Forging Paths Towards the Future

Pablo Marçal is a business visionary, always looking beyond the current horizon to anticipate market demands and needs.

Its approach to the future of business is permeated by the conviction that innovation is the engine that drives progress.

He not only sees innovation as a competitive advantage, but as a vital necessity for the survival and sustainable growth of any enterprise.

The Importance of Innovation

For Marçal, innovation is not a luxury, but a matter of survival.

He understands that, in an increasingly dynamic and unpredictable world, companies need to constantly adapt to stay relevant. This means being willing to challenge the status quo, question established practices, and embrace change as an opportunity for growth.

Staying Relevant in an Ever-Changing World

In an ever-evolving business environment, the ability to stay relevant is critical.

Marçal believes that the key to this lies in the ability to quickly adapt to market changes and anticipate future trends.

This requires an ongoing commitment to innovation and an open mindset to trying new ideas and approaches.

Insights for Future Success

For those who want to thrive in an ever-changing world, Marçal offers some valuable insights:

Be Open to Change: Instead of resisting change, embrace it as opportunities for growth and development.

Stay Aware of Trends: Always be aware of emerging trends and changes in the market so you can quickly adapt to new customer demands.

Cultivate a Culture of Innovation: Encourage creativity and innovative thinking throughout the organization by encouraging employees to contribute new ideas and solutions.

Be Agile and Flexible: Develop an agile and flexible mindset that allows you to respond quickly to market changes and adjust your strategy as needed.

Following these principles will not only help companies stay relevant in an ever-changing world, but also empower them to lead the way into the future, actively shaping the business landscape of tomorrow.

For Pablo Marçal, the future belongs to innovators - those who are willing to challenge the status quo and embrace the unknown with enthusiasm and determination.

Chapter 6:
Prosperity Mindset

Pablo Marçal is a passionate advocate of the power of the prosperity mindset - the belief that we are capable of attracting abundance in all areas of our lives through our mental attitudes and behaviors.

In this chapter, we will explore the attitudes necessary to attract prosperity, as taught by Pablo Marçal, and practical strategies for cultivating an abundance mindset in all areas of life.

1. **Gratitude and Appreciation**
One of the fundamental mental attitudes to attract prosperity is gratitude.

Pablo Marçal teaches us to value and appreciate everything we have in our lives, from the little things to the great achievements.

By cultivating a sense of gratitude, we make room for more blessings and opportunities to flow into our lives.

2. **Focus on Abundance**

Instead of focusing on scarcity and lack, Pablo Marçal encourages us to direct our attention to the abundance around us.

It reminds us that the universe is abundant by nature and that there is always more than enough to go around.

By adopting an abundance mindset, we are more open to receiving and sharing with others.

3. **Visualization and Manifestation**

Pablo Marçal is a big believer in the power of visualization and manifestation.

It teaches us to clearly visualize our goals and desires, and to cultivate feelings of joy and gratitude as if these things were already a reality in our lives.

By maintaining a positive and focused outlook on what we want to attract, we are more likely to manifest these things in our lives.

4. **Positive Action and Persistence**

A prosperity mindset is not just about thinking positively, it's also about acting positively.

Pablo Marçal reminds us of the importance of taking consistent and persistent steps towards

to our goals, even when we face challenges and obstacles.

He encourages us to maintain an attitude of confidence and determination, knowing that we can overcome any adversity on the path to prosperity.

5. **Detachment and Opening**

Finally, Pablo Marçal teaches us to practice detachment and to be open to receiving in unexpected ways.

He reminds us that sometimes we need to let go of our expectations and be open to new opportunities and possibilities that may present themselves in unexpected ways.

By remaining flexible and receptive, we allow prosperity to flow freely into our lives.

By cultivating a prosperity mindset based on gratitude, a focus on abundance, visualization and manifestation, positive action and persistence, and detachment and openness, we can attract more abundance and success in all areas of our lives.

6. **Constant Learning and Growth**

Pablo Marçal emphasizes the importance of continuous learning and personal growth to cultivate a prosperity mindset.

He encourages us to constantly seek new opportunities for development, whether through reading books, participating in courses, or interacting with inspiring people.

By investing in our own growth and expanding skills, we are opening doors to new possibilities for success and abundance.

7. **Elimination of Limiting Beliefs**

To attract true prosperity, Pablo Marçal challenges us to identify and overcome limiting beliefs that may be preventing us from reaching our full potential.

It teaches us to question these self-limiting beliefs and replace them with positive, empowering thoughts.

By actively challenging our limiting beliefs and reprogramming our minds for success, we can create a mental environment conducive to prosperity flowing freely.

8. **Networking and Positive Relationships**

Another fundamental aspect of the prosperity mindset is building a network of positive and supportive relationships.

Pablo Marçal encourages us to cultivate authentic and meaningful connections with others who share our values and aspirations.

These relationships can be a valuable source of support, inspiration, and collaborative opportunities, helping us expand our circle of influence and reach new levels of prosperity.

9. **Resilience and Adaptability**

Finally, Pablo Marçal reminds us of the importance of resilience and adaptability to face the challenges and uncertainties that will inevitably arise on our journey towards prosperity.

He encourages us to embrace change and see setbacks as opportunities for growth and learning.

By cultivating a resilient and adaptive mindset, we are able to overcome any adversity and continue moving towards our prosperity goals.

By incorporating these additional strategies into our prosperity mindset, we can create a solid foundation for attracting and manifesting abundance in all areas of our lives.

In the next chapters, we will explore how to apply these principles in the context of business and how we can create a culture of prosperity in our organizations, inspiring others to follow the same path in search of success and personal fulfillment.

Chapter 7
The Importance of Resilience

Pablo Marçal is a living example of the importance of resilience on the journey to success.

In this chapter, we'll explore lessons about resilience and overcoming challenges, inspired by her experience, as well as stories of perseverance and how to turn adversity into opportunities.

1. **Acceptance of Change**

Pablo Marçal teaches us that resilience begins with accepting change.

He shares how, throughout his career, he found himself in situations where he had to adapt to new environments, technologies and market demands.

Instead of resisting change, he embraced it, recognizing that the ability to adapt is essential to successfully face challenges.

2. **Focus on Solutions**

In the midst of difficulties, Pablo Marçal always focused on solutions instead of problems.

He reminds us that it's natural to face obstacles on the path to success, but what really matters is how we choose to deal with them.

By adopting a solution-oriented mindset, we are able to find creative and effective ways to overcome the challenges we face.

3. **Persistence and Determination**

Throughout his career, Pablo Marçal faced countless adversities that could have discouraged many others.

However, he demonstrated remarkable persistence and determination to press on, even when the odds were stacked against him.

He teaches us that success often requires a combination of talent, hard work, and an unwavering determination to never give up.

4. **Learning from Failure**

For Pablo Marçal, failure is not the end, but rather an opportunity for learning and growth.

He shares stories of times when he experienced failures and setbacks, but chose to view these experiences as valuable lessons that helped him become stronger and more resilient.

He reminds us that every obstacle is an opportunity to learn and develop.

5. **Cultivating a Positive Mindset**

Finally, Pablo Marçal emphasizes the importance of cultivating a positive mindset, even in the most challenging situations.

It teaches us that the way we choose to interpret events in our lives can have a significant impact on our ability to overcome adversity.

By maintaining a positive and hopeful attitude, we are able to face challenges with courage and determination.

By learning from Pablo Marçal's experience and applying these resilience lessons to our own lives, we can become more capable of overcoming the challenges and adversities we encounter on our path toward success and personal fulfillment.

6. **Transforming Adversities into Opportunities**

One of the most powerful lessons Pablo Marçal shares is the ability to transform adversity into opportunities.

He reminds us that it is often in the most difficult times that we find the greatest opportunities for growth and innovation.

Instead of being defeated by difficulties, Pablo Marçal encourages us to face them head on and look for creative ways to turn them into catalysts for success.

7. **Resistance to Discouragement**

Pablo Marçal demonstrates a remarkable resistance to discouragement, even when faced with seemingly insurmountable challenges.

He shares stories of times when he had to deal with significant setbacks in his life and career, but always found a way to pick himself up and move forward with renewed determination.

Your resilience inspires others to persevere in the face of adversity and believe that it is possible to overcome any obstacle.

8. **Community Support and Support Network**

Pablo Marçal recognizes the importance of community support and a strong support network to help you overcome challenges. He reminds us that we don't have to face difficulties alone and encourages us to seek support from friends, family, mentors, and co-workers. By sharing our struggles and seeking emotional and practical support, we can strengthen ourselves and find new perspectives to face challenges.

9. **Recognition of Inner Resilience**

Finally, Pablo Marçal teaches us that true resilience comes from within.

He encourages us to cultivate an inner foundation of strength, self-confidence, and self-determination that enables us to face challenges with courage and confidence.

By recognizing and nurturing our own inner resilience, we are able to overcome even the toughest challenges and emerge stronger than ever.

By incorporating these lessons about resilience into our lives, we can become more capable of facing challenges with courage, determination, and hope.

In the next chapters, we will explore how we can apply these resilience lessons to our businesses and all areas of our lives, empowering us to thrive even in the face of the most difficult circumstances.

Chapter 8:
Wealth: More than Money

Pablo Marçal offers deep insights into the true meaning of wealth, which goes beyond the purely financial aspects.

In this chapter, we will reflect on how to achieve a truly abundant life in all areas, not just the material.

1. **Abundance of Meaningful Relationships**

For Pablo Marçal, true wealth lies in the abundance of meaningful relationships.

He reminds us that the value of our lives cannot only be measured by our material achievements, but also by the emotional bonds we cultivate with others.

Genuine friendships, love and mutual support are invaluable sources of wealth that enrich our existence in profound and lasting ways.

2. **Health and Wellbeing**

Another fundamental aspect of true wealth is health and well-being.

Pablo Marçal teaches us that no matter how much money we have, without physical and mental health, our quality of life is severely compromised.

It encourages us to prioritize self-care by adopting healthy eating, exercise, sleep, and stress management habits.

By investing in our health and well-being, we are cultivating a valuable form of wealth that sustains us in all areas of our lives.

3. **Personal Growth and Spiritual Development**:

Pablo Marçal believes that true wealth also includes personal growth and spiritual development.

He invites us to constantly seek to expand our consciousness, deepening our self-knowledge and exploring questions of meaning and purpose in our lives.

By cultivating a deeper connection with ourselves and with something greater than ourselves, we discover a source of inner wealth that transcends material possessions.

4. **Contribution and Positive Impact**

Furthermore, Pablo Marçal highlights the importance of contribution and positive impact as essential aspects of true wealth.

He reminds us that by serving others and making a difference in their lives, we experience a deep sense of fulfillment and meaning.

Contributing to the well-being of our community and the world around us is a powerful way to enrich our own lives and create a lasting legacy of wealth.

5. **Balance and Harmony**

Finally, Pablo Marçal invites us to seek balance and harmony in all areas of our lives.

He teaches us that true wealth is not in accumulating excess in one area while neglecting others, but rather in finding a healthy balance between the different aspects of our existence - be it financial, emotional, physical or spiritual.

By cultivating this balance and harmony, we experience a deeper sense of fulfillment and satisfaction in our lives.

By taking a broader, more holistic view of wealth, we can create a truly abundant and meaningful life in all areas.

6. **Cultivation of Passions and Interests**

Pablo Marçal emphasizes the importance of cultivating passions and interests outside the professional or financial sphere.

He reminds us that true wealth also lies in finding joy and satisfaction in activities and hobbies that we are passionate about.

By making time to pursue our passions, we are nourishing our soul and enriching our experience of life in ways that go beyond monetary value.

7. **Lifestyle Flexibility and Freedom**

Furthermore, Pablo Marçal values lifestyle flexibility and freedom as essential components of true wealth.

It encourages us to seek a balance between work and play, allowing us to enjoy the freedom to choose how and where we spend our time.

By creating a lifestyle that allows us to enjoy meaningful moments with our loved ones and explore new experiences, we are truly living a rich and fulfilling life.

8. **Respect for the Environment and Nature**

Pablo Marçal also recognizes the importance of respecting the environment and nature as an integral part of true wealth.

It reminds us that our connection to the natural world is fundamental to our health and well-being, and that we must act responsibly to preserve and protect natural resources for future generations.

By living in harmony with the environment and appreciating the beauty of nature, we are enriching our life experience in profound and meaningful ways.

9. **Gratitude and Contentment**

Finally, Pablo Marçal invites us to cultivate an attitude of gratitude and contentment in our lives.

He teaches us that true wealth lies in appreciating and valuing what we have in the present, rather than constantly seeking more or comparing ourselves to others.

By cultivating a sense of gratitude for all the blessings in our lives, we are opening our hearts to a deeper, more meaningful experience of wealth in all its forms.

By adopting these principles of wealth beyond money, we can create a truly abundant and meaningful life in all areas.

In the next chapters, we'll explore how we can apply these principles to our businesses and our daily lives, empowering us to live with purpose, passion, and authenticity.

Chapter 9:
The Role of Education and Continuous Learning

Pablo Marçal recognizes the importance of education and personal development as fundamental pillars on the journey towards success.

In this chapter, we will explore the significance of continuous learning and the search for knowledge, according to the teachings of Pablo Marçal, in addition to presenting recommendations for books, courses and resources to expand our understanding and improve our skills.

1. **Investment in Yourself**

Pablo Marçal emphasizes that investing in our own education and personal development is one of the best ways to achieve success.

It reminds us that our knowledge and skills are valuable assets that we can cultivate and develop throughout our lives, giving us a competitive advantage in the job market and in achieving our personal goals.

2. **Growth Mindset**

According to Pablo Marçal, adopting a growth mindset is essential for continuous learning and personal development.

He encourages us to see challenges as opportunities for growth and believe in our potential to learn and evolve over time.

By cultivating a growth mindset, we are open to exploring new ideas, trying new experiences, and expanding our horizons.

3. **Reading as a Development Tool**

For Pablo Marçal, reading is one of the most powerful ways to expand our knowledge and perspective on the world.

He recommends that we regularly dedicate time to reading inspiring, educational and informative books, which allow us to learn from the wisdom accumulated over the centuries and inspire us to reach new heights in our lives.

4. **Specific Courses and Training**

In addition to reading, Pablo Marçal encourages participation in specific courses and training related to our interests and objectives.

Whether through online courses, in-person workshops or professional development programs, he reminds us that formal, hands-on education is an effective way to acquire new skills, deepen our understanding and stay up to date with the latest trends in our field.

5. **Networking and Interpersonal Learning**

Pablo Marçal also highlights the importance of networking and interpersonal learning as an integral part of our educational and personal development journey.

It encourages us to seek meaningful connections with other professionals, mentors, and coworkers who can share their insights, experiences, and knowledge with us.

By collaborating with others and sharing ideas, we expand our understanding and enrich our own learning journey.

6. **Exploring New Experiences**

For Pablo Marçal, learning is not limited to the formal classroom environment or reading books.

It encourages us to actively seek out new experiences and challenges that can expand our horizons and broaden our understanding of the world.

By exposing ourselves to different cultures, perspectives and practices, we enrich our knowledge repertoire and develop a more open and flexible mind.

7. **Mentoring and Guidance**

Another valuable resource for continued learning is mentorship and guidance from experienced and successful individuals in our areas of interest.

Pablo Marçal highlights the importance of seeking mentors who can guide us, share their experiences and offer practical advice to help us achieve our goals.

By learning from the wisdom and insights of mentors, we accelerate our own development and evolution process.

8. **Harness of Technology**

In today's digital world, technology offers a multitude of resources and tools for continuous learning.

Pablo Marçal encourages us to make the most of these technologies, from online learning platforms to educational apps and podcasts.

He reminds us that knowledge is within our reach, and that technology can be a powerful ally on our journey of self-development.

9. **Learning through Failure**

Finally, Pablo Marçal reminds us that failure is also a valuable learning opportunity.

He encourages us to embrace challenges and setbacks as an inevitable part of the growth process, and to learn from our mistakes and experiences.

By facing failure with resilience and determination, we transform each obstacle into an opportunity for personal growth and improvement.

By taking a proactive approach to continuous learning and personal development, we can empower ourselves to achieve our goals and create a life of meaning, success and fulfillment.

In the next chapters, we will explore how we can apply these principles to our businesses and all areas of our lives, empowering us to reach our full potential and live a truly extraordinary life.

Chapter 10
Leadership and Entrepreneurship

Pablo Marçal shares valuable insights into effective leadership and successful entrepreneurship, based on his vast experience.

In this chapter, we will explore the essential leadership principles that can be applied in different contexts, inspired by the vision of Pablo Marçal.

1. **Vision and Purpose**

According to Pablo Marçal, an effective leader is one who has a clear vision and an inspiring purpose.

He teaches us that vision is what guides a leader's actions and decisions, while purpose is what motivates and energizes his team.

By articulating a compelling vision and aligning organizational goals with a greater purpose, a leader can inspire and mobilize others in pursuit of common goals.

2. **Empathy and Communication**

For Pablo Marçal, empathy and effective communication are fundamental pillars of leadership.

It reminds us of the importance of listening carefully to team members' concerns and perspectives, demonstrating empathy and understanding.

Furthermore, it highlights the need to communicate clearly and transparently, sharing relevant information and maintaining an open line of communication at all levels of the organization.

3. **Team Development**

Pablo Marçal emphasizes the importance of investing in team development as an essential part of leadership.

It encourages us to identify and cultivate talent, providing opportunities for learning and professional growth.

By empowering and inspiring team members to reach their full potential, a leader creates a dynamic and productive work environment where everyone can contribute meaningfully to collective success.

4. **Resilience and Adaptability**

In a world in constant change, Pablo Marçal highlights the importance of resilience and adaptability in leadership.

It reminds us that challenges and setbacks are inevitable, but what really matters is how we respond to them.

By demonstrating resilience and adaptability in the face of adversity, a leader instills trust and confidence in his or her team, creating an environment where everyone can thrive even in difficult times.

5. **Innovation and Creativity**

Finally, Pablo Marçal believes that effective leadership requires a commitment to innovation and creativity.

It encourages us to constantly seek new ways to approach problems and opportunities, encouraging an environment of creative thinking and experimentation.

By fostering a culture of innovation, a leader inspires his team to challenge the status quo and seek innovative solutions to the challenges they face.

By incorporating these leadership principles into their daily practices, leaders can create more resilient, adaptable and innovative organizations capable of meeting the challenges and opportunities of the contemporary business world.

6. **Decision Making and Responsibility**

Pablo Marçal highlights the importance of assertive decision-making and personal responsibility in leadership and entrepreneurship.

He emphasizes that leaders must be able to make difficult decisions with confidence and act responsibly for the results.

By taking responsibility for their choices and actions, leaders instill confidence in their teams and establish a standard of accountability that permeates the entire organization.

7. **Mentoring and Development of Future Leaders**

In addition to leading in the present, Pablo Marçal highlights the importance of mentoring and developing future leaders.

He believes that leaders must invest in the growth and development of other team members, enabling them to take on leadership roles and contribute to long-term organizational success.

By cultivating a culture of leadership and talent development, leaders create a lasting legacy of excellence and positive impact.

8. **Integrity and Ethics**

Integrity and ethics are fundamental values for Pablo Marçal when it comes to leadership and entrepreneurship.

It emphasizes the importance of acting honestly, transparently and ethically in all business interactions and decisions.

By demonstrating integrity and ethics in all their actions, leaders build trust with their employees, customers and partners, strengthening their organizations' long-term reputation and success.

9. **Sustainable Vision and Social Impact**

Finally, Pablo Marçal believes that leaders must adopt a sustainable vision and consider the social impact of their business decisions and activities.

It encourages us to seek opportunities to create a positive impact on society and the environment by aligning business objectives with broader social and environmental concerns.

By incorporating a sustainable and socially responsible business approach, leaders not only generate financial results, but also contribute to a better, more equitable world.

By following these principles of leadership and entrepreneurship, leaders can create truly inspiring and impactful organizations capable of driving long-term success and making a difference in the world.

In the next chapters, we will explore how we can apply these principles to our own endeavors and personal leadership, empowering us to reach our full potential and create lasting positive impact.

Chapter 11
Social Impact and Corporate Responsibility

Pablo Marçal offers an inspiring vision about the role of companies in society and the importance of assuming social responsibilities.

In this chapter, we'll explore his perspective on how companies can make a difference in the world, as well as provide examples of corporate initiatives that have a significant positive impact.

1. **Purpose Beyond Profit**

For Pablo Marçal, companies have a crucial role not only in generating profit, but also in creating positive social impact.

He believes that companies must have a purpose beyond profit, seeking to contribute to the well-being of society and the environment in which they operate.

By aligning their business objectives with broader social concerns, companies can become agents of positive change and promote a more just and sustainable world.

2. **Corporate Social Responsibility (CSR)**

Pablo Marçal advocates the importance of corporate social responsibility (CSR) as a strategic approach to incorporating social and environmental considerations into all areas of a company's operation.

It highlights that companies must take responsibility for their impact on communities, the environment, customers, employees and other stakeholders, seeking to create shared value for everyone involved.

3. **Sustainable and Environmental Practices**

One of the ways companies can have a positive social impact is through adopting sustainable and environmental practices.

Pablo Marçal encourages companies to reduce their carbon footprint, minimize waste and pollution, and conserve natural resources.

He highlights that sustainable practices not only benefit the environment, but also generate operational efficiencies, reduce costs and strengthen the company's reputation.

4. **Inclusion and Diversity**

Pablo Marçal emphasizes the importance of inclusion and diversity in the workplace as a way to promote equity and social justice.

He believes companies should strive to create inclusive work environments where all people feel valued, respected and empowered to contribute fully.

By promoting diversity across gender, ethnicity, sexual orientation and socioeconomic background, companies can reap the benefits of a more creative, innovative and engaged workforce.

5. **Social Investment and Philanthropy**

In addition to its business operations, Pablo Marçal encourages companies to invest in social initiatives and philanthropy programs that address pressing societal challenges.

He highlights that companies have unique resources and influence that can be directed toward important causes such as education, healthcare, anti-poverty and community development.

By actively engaging in the community and supporting nonprofit organizations, companies can make a tangible difference in people's lives and the world at large.

Examples of companies that have embraced these principles and are making a difference include Patagonia, known for its sustainable practices and commitment to the environment; Microsoft, which invests in inclusion and skills development programs; and Unilever, which has adopted a comprehensive approach to sustainability across its supply chain.

By adopting a business approach centered on purpose and social responsibility, companies can become agents of positive change and create a lasting impact on society and the environment.

6. **Social Innovation and Impact Entrepreneurship**

Pablo Marçal also highlights the importance of social innovation and impact entrepreneurship as drivers of positive change in society.

It encourages companies to take an innovative approach to solving social and environmental problems, identifying business opportunities that generate financial returns and social impact simultaneously.

By supporting social entrepreneurs and investing in innovative solutions to pressing issues, companies can catalyze transformative change and create a fairer, more sustainable world for all.

7. **Transparency and Accountability**

Another essential aspect of corporate responsibility, according to Pablo Marçal, is transparency and accountability.

It emphasizes that companies must be transparent about their business practices, social and environmental impacts, allowing stakeholders to evaluate their performance and make informed decisions.

Additionally, it highlights the importance of accountability, encouraging companies to take responsibility for their mistakes and actions, and to work to correct any harm caused.

8. **Collaboration and Strategic Partnerships**

Pablo Marçal believes that collaboration and strategic partnerships are fundamental to face the most complex social and environmental challenges.

It encourages companies to collaborate with governments, civil society organizations, academia and other businesses to maximize their impact and achieve more meaningful results.

By joining forces with other public and private sector actors, companies can leverage complementary resources and diverse expertise to address issues more effectively and comprehensively.

9. **Organizational Culture and Shared Values**

Finally, Pablo Marçal highlights the importance of a strong organizational culture and shared values as a basis for corporate responsibility.

It encourages companies to cultivate a culture that values ethics, integrity and a commitment to the well-being of society, incorporating these values into all their operations and decisions.

By creating a culture of responsibility and social impact, companies can inspire and mobilize their employees, customers and other stakeholders to unite behind a common goal of creating a better world for all.

These corporate responsibility principles, when embodied genuinely and holistically, not only benefit society and the environment, but also strengthen companies in the long term by promoting sustainability, resilience and shared prosperity.

In the next chapters, we will explore how leaders can translate these principles into tangible actions in their organizations and communities, empowering themselves to lead with purpose, passion, and impact.

Chapter 12
Implementing the Teachings of Pablo Marçal

In this final chapter, we will explore a practical guide for readers to apply Pablo Marçal's valuable teachings to their own lives and businesses.

We will offer concrete strategies to transform knowledge into action and achieve tangible results, following the principles and insights shared by Pablo Marçal throughout this book.

1. **Self-knowledge and Reflection**

The first step to implementing Pablo Marçal's teachings is to dedicate time to self-awareness and reflection.

We encourage readers to pause and honestly evaluate their own strengths, weaknesses, values, and goals. Identifying areas for growth and setting clear goals is essential to beginning the journey of personal and professional transformation.

2. **Define a Purpose and Vision**

Inspired by Pablo Marçal's emphasis on purpose and vision, readers are encouraged to define their own mission and vision for their lives and businesses. Establishing a meaningful purpose and inspiring vision provides an internal compass to guide daily decisions and actions, creating a sense of direction and purpose.

3. **Develop an Action Plan**

Based on the established goals and vision, readers are invited to develop a clear and achievable action plan.

This plan must include specific steps, defined deadlines and resources necessary to achieve the outlined objectives.

By breaking big goals into smaller, more manageable tasks, it becomes easier to stay focused and motivated along the way.

4. **Practice Empathy and Communication**

Inspired by Pablo Marçal's emphasis on empathy and effective communication, readers are encouraged to cultivate positive, collaborative relationships in their personal and professional lives. This includes actively listening, being open to feedback, expressing gratitude, and building authentic connections with others.

Clear and empathetic communication is essential for building solid relationships and cohesive teams.

5. **Invest in Personal and Professional Development**

Pablo Marçal values investment in personal and professional development as a path to continuous growth.

Readers are encouraged to seek out learning opportunities such as courses, workshops, reading, and mentoring that will help them acquire new skills, expand their knowledge, and achieve their goals.

6. **Act with Integrity and Responsibility**

Following the principles of integrity and responsibility defended by Pablo Marçal, readers are urged to act honestly, transparently and ethically in all areas of their lives and businesses.

Taking responsibility for your actions and fulfilling your commitments strengthens trust and respect from others, building lasting relationships and a solid reputation.

7. **Seek Social Impact Opportunities**

Inspired by Pablo Marçal's vision for social impact and corporate responsibility, readers are encouraged to seek opportunities to contribute positively to their communities and the world at large.

This can include volunteering, donating to social causes, supporting local initiatives and aligning your business with social and environmental responsibility values.

8. **Persistence and Resilience**

Finally, readers are reminded of the importance of persistence and resilience throughout their journey of implementing Pablo Marçal's teachings.

The path to success can be filled with challenges and obstacles, but it is determination and the ability to bounce back from setbacks that truly drive progress.

By remaining persistent and resilient in the face of adversity, readers can overcome any obstacle and achieve their most ambitious goals.

By following this practical guide and applying Pablo Marçal's teachings to their lives and businesses, readers are empowered to create a lasting positive impact, achieve success, and live with purpose and passion.

May this journey of personal and professional transformation be full of learning and growth.

Epilogue
Towards a New Journey

As we reach the end of this book, we hope you have been inspired by the teachings and insights shared by Pablo Marçal.

Your journey through the pages of this book was just the beginning of an exciting journey toward personal growth, professional success, and positive impact on the world.

Remember that implementing Pablo Marçal's teachings is not just about absorbing knowledge, but transforming it into action.

Every concept, principle, and strategy discussed throughout this book has the power to catalyze significant change in your life and business, as long as you are willing to put them into practice.

As you prepare to embark on this new journey, keep the following principles in mind:

- Cultivate self-knowledge and constant reflection, as they are the key to unlocking your true potential.

- Define a purpose and inspiring vision that guide your actions and inspire you to achieve great things.

- Be an empathetic, communicative and ethical leader, both in your personal and professional relationships.

- Constantly seek learning and development opportunities, staying up to date with trends and innovations in your field.

- Commit to social and environmental responsibility by looking for ways to contribute positively to your community and the world at large.

- Remain resilient and persistent, even in the face of the challenges and setbacks you will inevitably encounter on your journey.

Always remember that success is not only measured by material achievements, but also by the positive impact you leave on the world and the lives of those around you.

By following Pablo Marçal's teachings and incorporating them into your own journey, you are positioning yourself to achieve great things and create a meaningful legacy that will last for generations.

May this journey of self-discovery, growth and impact be filled with joy, inspiration and fulfillment.

May you continue to thrive and evolve, always striving to be the best version of yourself and making a difference wherever you go.

Now, it's time to move on and start your own journey towards a bright future full of possibilities.

May this book be just the beginning of an exciting and transformative journey that will take you to places you never thought possible.

Thank you for accompanying us on this journey.

May your journey be extraordinary and may you always find inspiration, courage and wisdom to move forward.

With gratitude and best wishes,

Elean Bolandine

www.ingramcontent.com/pod-product-compliance
Lightning Source LLC
Chambersburg PA
CBHW050236230526
45470CB00005B/1986